Capture the Spotlight

Improve Your Presentation Skills and
Make Public Speaking Your Competitive Edge

By Narges Nirumvala

This book is available at special discounts to use as premiums and sales pro-
motions, or for use in corporate training programs. For this and volume
discounts, contact the author through the website: http://www.capturethe
spotlight.com.

Cover photo by Kris Krug

First published by Dog Ear Publishing
4010 W. 86th Street, Ste H
Indianapolis, IN 46268
www.dogearpublishing.net

ISBN: 978-1-4575-1871-3

This book is printed on acid-free paper.

Printed in the United States of America

Dedication

This book is dedicated with love and gratitude to my mother,
A wonderful woman who made everything possible.
Thank you for believing in me and helping me find my voice.

"When you are inspired by some great purpose, some extraordinary project, all your thoughts break their bonds: Your mind transcends limitations, your consciousness expands in every direction, and you find yourself in a new, great, and wonderful world. Dormant forces, faculties, and talents become alive, and your discover yourself to be a greater person by far than you ever dreamed yourself to be."

—Patanjali

Contents

Preface

"Books constitute capital. A library book lasts as long as a house, for hundreds of years. It is not, then, an article of mere consumption but fairly of capital, and often in the case of professional men, setting out in life, it is their only capital. "

—Thomas Jefferson

This book is born out of sitting through hundreds of boring meetings and tedious presentations by otherwise exceptional people. One day in particular stands out in my mind; I was looking forward to a half-day seminar by an IT executive (a real innovator in his field) at a local association. I remember walking into the hotel ballroom and finding a table to sit at. I introduced myself to the other people at the table, sipped my water, and eagerly awaited his insights and wisdom. What a huge letdown it was when he actually started talking. He was so nervous he kept reading from his overhead slides and had the most monotone voice. We had hours of this to look forward to! The neighbor to my left started leaning on her arm on the table and slowly fell asleep; her head eventually hitting the table with a soft thud, which jolted her awake. The neighbor to my right was on her cell phone texting and surfing the net the whole time. He had lost the audience. In an attempt to stay awake and alert, I started writing down all the ways he could have improved his presentation on my napkin. Months later I found that napkin and thought, *Wow,*

I have some great material here; I should do something with this. It's now more than a year later and that napkin became the basis for this book!

If you've bought this book, then, like that IT executive, you are probably a successful individual in your own right, but you have one huge advantage on him: *You know that you could improve your public speaking skills and want to have complete mastery in this area.* This book is a good place to start. If these principles are applied correctly and consistently, they will have a positive impact on your communication skills and ultimately up level your life.

Acknowledgments

"Gratitude bestows reverence, allowing us to encounter everyday epiphanies, those transcendent moments of awe that change forever how we experience life and the world."
—John Milton

I am so grateful to God for all the blessings in my life. This book has been a dream for many years, and there are so many people who helped me make it a reality.

First, I want to thank my parents, who have supported me throughout my life and who believe in me so unequivocally. My father gave me a strong business sense from an early age and taught me how to see things from the entrepreneur's point of view—something that has been invaluable in my life. My mother gave me a compassionate heart and the desire to give back to the community and use my gift to make a difference in the world.

I also want to thank my amazingly patient husband, who put up with all the late nights of writing and hours of "What do you think of this book title?" "Are you listening to me?" and "What about this chapter heading?" He has been a tremendous support and sounding board to me throughout the whole writing and publishing process. To my little one, who came into my life only a few years ago, but who transformed it so completely: being a mom has taught me so much about myself and given me a priceless gift. I cannot imagine my life without you both.

To the community leaders who have inspired me and shared their wisdom with me over the years—thank you. Finally I want to thank all my family, friends, mentors, sponsors, and colleagues for their support over the years. A huge debt of gratitude also goes to my wonderful clients who so often said to me during coaching sessions, "You should write a book about this!" You have given me the confidence to write this book.

Thank you all for giving me your love and encouragement again and again. I appreciate every kind word and action that has propelled me to this moment. God bless you all.

—Narges P. Nirumvala
Vancouver, British Columbia

Introduction

Y ou will find this book full of tools, tips, and strategies that will help you improve your presentation skills and be a more dynamic and powerful public speaker. I want to give you a handy and practical guide that you can keep with you and turn to in a whole variety of speaking situations. I have intentionally kept the information concise, and organized it into bite-sized chunks, so it's easy to read and digest. It also means that if you're busy like me (and I bet you are!), you can dip into the book anytime and immediately find useful information that you can apply the same day.

"You see, being able to speak in public gives your thoughts and emotions life. It will bring you out of the shadows and into the light."

There is no fluff, filler, or unnecessary long stories or examples traditionally used to pad out books. (I hate those in business books and always skip them anyway.) **This book is just 100 percent pure, distilled, useful information born out of my years of experience as an executive speech coach, keynote speaker, and presentation skills trainer.**

I've also written this book with the entrepreneurial approach in mind, because that's how I think. However, it doesn't matter if you're a CEO or a high school student—if you're a go-getter and an innovator, someone who wants to take charge of the way you communicate and respond to situations so you always use them to your advantage and make the best possible impression, then this book is for you.

My Story

I need you to think back to when you were in school. Were you in or out? Cool or nerdy? Those years define so much of how we feel about ourselves. Remember that quiet, weird kid standing alone in the dark corner of the playground looking depressed all the time? That was me. I had a horrendous time at school—I was bullied and teased all the time about everything. I was painfully insecure and felt so alone in the world. What turned around my life was finding my voice, both in writing and in speaking. I was slowly able to share my thoughts and opinions with the world. It changed my life.

Today I'm a successful and confident businesswoman, in large part because of my ability to communicate. But I haven't forgotten that scared little girl and how difficult those days were. They made me the person I am today—so I'm grateful to her for her strength through all the hard times. The world is full of people living in fear and doubt—afraid of speaking their minds, not wanting to be in the spotlight or make a fool of themselves. But just like I used to—they hide it so no one really knows how they feel. Well, I know how that feels and this book is written for the scared child in you.

You see, being able to speak in public gives your thoughts and emotions life. It will bring you out of the shadows and into the light. Once I found my voice, I slowly began to realize that I had power over my own destiny. **Public speaking gives you power and energy—it's like a life force starts flowing through you that fuels each of your cells with confidence and vitality, so you are able to shine from within.** That's what it does for me, and I know that if you apply the principles in this book correctly and consistently, it can do the same for you.

How to Use This Book

You must do more than just read this book to transform your communication skills—you have to apply what's in this book, too. You must take action, not procrastinate, not find excuses, just start. There are five sections to this book—here's a quick breakdown of what you can expect.

• Part One: Skill Building and Training

The first section is the foundation you must have to be a good public speaker. It focuses on helping you build fundamental skills – everyone must master these. We will not go into them in detail, it's just not possible in a book of this length, but it will be a good beginning. Some of the concepts are so important (such as good eye contact) that I will repeat them from one chapter to another in different contexts to re-enforce the message.

• Part Two: Coaching Moments

The second section focuses on giving you coaching points for the more intangible aspects of communication – from saying 'NO' to confronting your fear. Not all of these are directly related to public speaking, but they come up so often with my clients that I put them in to help you.

• Part Three: Public Speaking in Real Life

The third section gives you tips for real life situations where you need to have great public speaking skills. From giving a speech at a wedding or accepting an award – it's here.

• Part Four: Pulling It All Together

This section is one chapter and related exercises to help create and implement a plan of action to pull everything you've learnt in the book together.

• Part Five: Quick Tip Sheets

Here you'll find five one-page tip sheets for various situations—you'll want to use them again and again. I wish I had had something like this when I started out!

"You must take action, not procrastinate, not find excuses, just start."

At the end of every chapter in the first three sections are exercises, so you can think about what you've read and put it into practice. Sometimes you'll be asked to be introspective, sometimes you'll need to do something—either way it's essential to carry these out if you want to make the most of this book.

My goal in writing this book is ultimately to help you fully realize your potential as a speaker and captivate everyone who hears you. It's my life's work and I'm honored to share it with you. At the end of this book, in the "About the Author" section, you'll see how to keep in touch with me—

please do take advantage of it and let me know how the book helped you and what you would like to see in the next edition. I want this book to be the first chapter in a dialogue between us. So sit down and enjoy!

Coaching Exercise—Introduction

1. How often do you get the opportunity to speak or present in your current position?

2. If you were a better speaker, how would it impact your career?

3. If you had a higher profile as a result of more speaking opportunities and greater confidence as a presenter, how would this impact the bottom line of your organization?

PART ONE

SKILL BUILDING AND TRAINING

CHAPTER 1

Why Public Speaking?

"Knowing others is intelligence; knowing yourself is true wisdom. Mastering others is strength; mastering yourself is true power."

—Laozi

As I'm writing this chapter it's almost Valentine's Day, and all around me I can see that we turn our attention to matters of the heart. One of the great passions of my life is public speaking—not only because it gives you the ability to express yourself, but also because of its transformative powers. Here are seven reasons why public speaking can change your life and lead to greater success in business.

1. It is at the heart of leadership development.

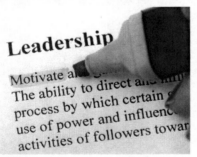

If you look at any great leader in history, you find that at their heart is a powerful communicator. Their ability to speak impacts their ability to inspire and motivate their people, delegate effectively, and influence others to take action. Public speaking is at the core of leadership development and will directly impact the range of your influence and the height of your success. Perhaps you're thinking, *But I'm not a leader.* I have to respectfully disagree. I believe that everyone is a leader of some kind—an expert in

8

your field, a volunteer at your church, a manager at work, the head of a committee, the president of your class, or the CEO of a company—it all takes leadership. The title changes, but the guts of it remain the same. *I recommend you read Robin Sharma's book on leadership listed in the recommended reading list at the back of this book—it's all about the true nature of leadership.*

2. It gets you out of your comfort zone.

To get out of your comfort zone, you must confront life and force yourself to go beyond the boundaries of what you would normally do. This, by its very nature, is scary. Don't let your fear of public speaking hold you back from the potential success it may bring now or in the future. Who knows one day who will be sitting in the audience listening to you speak—it may open a door to an opportunity you wouldn't have had otherwise.

> *"Public speaking is at the core of leadership development and will directly impact the range of your influence and the height of your success."*

3. It increases your visibility.

This is one of the biggest benefits public speaking can bring, and yet so few people realize it. If you want to stand out from the others in your industry or the company you work for, then public speaking is the way to do it. But remember, sometimes people are not ready for the attention it brings—something to reflect upon as you read this book.

4. It builds your confidence.

Confidence is at the heart of anything great that you do. Public speaking has the ability to build your confidence in leaps and bounds. Once you discover the confidence you have within yourself through public speaking, you'll see how it transforms every aspect of your life, as it did with me.

5.   It acts as a creative outlet.

Public speaking is as much an art as a science. Just watch any great live theatrical performance, such as a Shakespearean monologue, and you'll see that. If you allow public speaking to be part of your creative pallet, it will help transform your business into a masterpiece.

6.   It's a great marketing tool.

If you're like me and are passionate about what you do, then you will want to share it with the world. What better way to do that than to create a keynote speech, or run a seminar or workshop about it? Many of my professional clients, such as mortgage brokers, financial planners, and lawyers, are running seminars and workshops (with my help, of course) for the very first time to great success. Running educational events is one of the best ways to promote your business or raise your profile at work.

"Confidence is at the heart of anything great that you do. Public speaking has the ability to build your confidence in leaps and bounds."

---

7.   It builds your brand profile.

This point is maximizing your brand presence in the marketplace. The more you speak, the more you're out there, the more powerful your brand presence. The topic of your keynote and the way you deliver it can also influence the way people perceive your brand. This can be a powerful tool for any organization, but especially big ones. Your C-level executives should be actively speaking and getting positive exposure for your brand.

So whether you love Valentine's Day, or think it's just another overcommercialized holiday, we can at least agree that doing what you love is one of life's greatest gifts. This year, why not take your business or career to the next level by harnessing the power of public speaking? It's going to be up to you to apply the principles in the following chapters and make them part of your life.

Coaching Exercise 1

1. Are you comfortable being the center of attention? Yes No

2. If no, why not?

3. What aspects of public speaking make you uncomfortable or do you find particularly challenging?

4. What do you hope to gain by reading this book? List three desired outcomes.

    a.

    b.

    c.

CHAPTER 2

Public Speaking 101: Basics to Build On

"You were born with wings, why prefer to crawl through life?"

—Rumi

Let's start with the fundamental skills that you must have in your pubic speaking arsenal to succeed. I say *fundamental,* but the truth is that many people never master the basics and it shows in every presentation they make. In fact, I have found that coaching people in the basics is actually more difficult than the advanced stuff, because people don't think it's important or they get embarrassed.

Many people don't realize how complex public speaking is and how many different things a public speaking coach works on when they are training a client. In this chapter I want to take you through ten absolutely fundamental things—the foundations of good speaking. Sometimes when I'm working with a client, the best place to begin is with the basics. Please remember that, like any of the other tips and strategies I share with you in this book, you must implement them to see a change in your performance. If you just read it and forget it, nothing will change and your public speaking skills will not improve. So here we go.

1. Preparation

I'm surprised how many of my clients just wing it through presentations without doing the necessary research and really planning out what they want to say. So the first step is to sit down and think about what you want to achieve, then work backward. What outcomes do you want from this presentation? Then write it down (or type it out—I have the worst handwriting, so I type almost everything!). Research any information you need to flesh out online and reference that in your notes. For my executive clients, I even recommend that they research the people who will be in the room for closed-door, boardroom presentations.

2. Organization

You're going to begin by organizing what you want to say. It sounds simple, right? Then why is it that so many people sound lost or confused when they begin to speak in public? Imagine that your thoughts are a filing cabinet—are they stuffed full of papers just thrown in, or are they in files clearly labeled in alphabetical order?

3. Words and Vocabulary

The words you choose can make all the difference in the world when you speak. They can bring life to your words or bore people to death. So choose them wisely when writing your speech or even when you need to do impromptu speaking. Here are two quick examples.

A manager speaks to motivate her team: "I am determined that we are going to…" versus "We are going to be unstoppable when we…". The second sentence is much more powerful.

An executive giving a report on earnings: "This quarter we were paying attention to…" versus "This quarter we were focused on..." The second sentence is more concise and, again, more powerful.

4.   Voice Projection

A couple of months ago I heard an author speak at an event. She was speaking at a book launch event—obviously she was a very talented writer, but I could barely hear what she was saying and that was *with* a microphone. Yes, that's right, she was barely audible even with a microphone. That's why it's essential to have good vocal projection. You must be able to literally throw your voice to the back of any room you'll be speaking in.

5.   Voice Tone/Pitch

Imagine that your voice is a landscape. Is it flat like a valley, or undulating with hills and mountains? Ideally you want valleys and mountains. Your voice should go up and down. Lack of variety in pitch is one big reason why people sound boring when they speak. You need to make your voice more interesting so people actually want to listen to you, not fall asleep.

"Public speaking is your way of communicating your brilliance with the world. It's not enough to be passionate or knowledgeable about your area of expertise; you need to be able to express yourself eloquently, so your audience can touch your mind through your words."

---

6.   Pace

Depending on the subject matter and context of your speech or presentation, you should vary the pace (or speed) of your speaking. So, for example, on the radio you would go faster—you sound better on the radio at a fast pace. If you're giving a technical presentation to a lay audience, then slow down so people can really absorb the information. If you're doing an inspirational keynote, you will need to vary the pace according to what you're saying and move the audience's emotions along with you.

7.   Gestures

What do I do with my hands? This is a question I get all the time. Some things *not* to do with your hands include put them in your pockets, play with your hair, rub the sweat off your palms on your clothes (yes, I've seen that!), rub your hands together like you're trying to make fire...phew, I'm tired just thinking about this list. Use your hands to communicate, not groom yourself!! Also remember that the gestures you use should be tailored to the type of speaking—so more animated gestures for a keynote, more tame for a television interview, and more simple and meaningful for if speaking while sitting at a boardroom table.

8.   Eye Contact

Your eyes are the way you connect with your audience—whether it's an audience of ten or ten thousand. How do you feel? Are you nervous? Are you excited? What are you really thinking about? Do you want to be speaking, or would you rather be somewhere else? Your audience will feel the answers through your eyes—so be careful and focus your thoughts and emotions on the moment.

9.   Posture

Do you have good posture? I talk a lot about posture in my writing, and I know you might get sick of it at some point—but it's because good posture equals confidence, and it commands attention much better than bad posture. Some signs that you *don't* have good posture—you're slouching, leaning, hip sitting, or hunched over. So stand up straight!

10. Humor

Every time I hear a speech, whether it's at a board of trade function or a conference, it inevitably starts with a joke—you know, the type you find on the Internet. In my humble opinion, the worst thing you can do is start your speech with a joke. It does not mean you'll be funny or that anyone will laugh...in fact, they might laugh *at* you rather than *with* you. Humor should be more natural and rooted in your real life. So look to your life and tell them a true story—you'll be surprised how funny you can be.

We've now gone through the basics of good public speaking. Now it's up to you—pick one topic and work on it. The next time you're standing up to give a presentation, whether it's a sales pitch or a keynote, be aware of these elements and see where you can improve. As I've said before, my goal is to help you become a better, more confident speaker. On stage every flaw becomes magnified many times over and people notice every nuance, so you need to make good habits second nature to you. Public speaking is your way to communicating your brilliance with the world. It's not enough to be passionate or knowledgeable about your area of expertise; you need to be able to express yourself eloquently, so your audience can touch your mind through your words.

Coaching Exercise 2

1. Of the ten fundamentals listed, which one is your strongest?

2. What can you do to build on this area?

3. Which one is your weakest and needs the most work? Be honest!

4. What can you do to work on this area?

CHAPTER 3

Body Language Secrets of Confident Businesspeople

"If we did all the things we are capable of doing, we would literally astound ourselves."

—Thomas A. Edison

You walk into a room full of people you've never met before. Someone hands you a "Hello, my name is" badge and away you go. As you walk around the room deciding whom to speak to first, you notice people looking at you. What do they think when they see you? If only you could read minds, it would be so much easier! When people meet you for the very first time, do you make a positive first impression? Do people think, *Wow, that's a confident person?*

Remember, people are making assumptions about who you are and what you do, before you've ever said a single word. It takes seconds, not minutes, to make a good first impression, so pay attention! Of course they notice your hair, makeup, and the way you dress. In addition to that, you are sending out, like radar, subtle nonverbal cues through your body language. Here are five ways to send out the right signals.

1. Eye Contact

Making eye contact across a crowded room isn't just reserved for romantic novels. In any business situation, the ability to make eye contact is essential to a strong business presence. When you make eye contact you show that you are

listening to that person and that you care about what they have to say, even if you don't agree with it (*particularly* if you don't agree with it). Eye contact is a show of strength and confidence.

2. Smile

People don't think of smiling as body language. But your face is part of your body, isn't it? **You communicate your passion for what you do and your joy for life through your smile.** All other things being equal, would you rather do business with someone who looks miserable or happy? Make sure the first thing they see about you is a big, ostentatious smile. You love who you are and it shows!

3. Good Posture

Remember when your mother used to tell you to sit up straight? Well, she was right. Slouching, scrunching, and leaning send out all the wrong signals. So stand up straight with your shoulders back and head up. You're not an overworked cave dweller; you're a powerful, confident individual.

4. A Strong Handshake

A firm, confident handshake is one of the first things people will notice about you when they finally do speak with you. Limp-wristed men and women don't make the best first impression. If you do have a weak handshake, then grab hold of your significant other and practice, practice, practice! A firm handshake says, *I know who I am and I'm happy to meet you.*

"You are a successful, powerful person and it should ooze out of your every pore before you've said a single word."

5. Stop Fidgeting

Powerful people don't fidget. Fidgeting could include playing with your hair, picking at your nails, rubbing your face, or any other nervous habit. It makes you look bored and weak. Often fidgeting is unconscious, so you may need to ask someone close to you to observe you and take action accordingly. If you need to do something to keep yourself occupied in a particularly dull meeting, then why not take notes, or ask a question. If you're bored at a networking event, then treat yourself to a glass of wine or excuse yourself and walk up to someone new.

You are a successful, powerful person and it should ooze out of your every pore before you've said a single word. Understanding the nuances of good body language is one way that you can control other people's perceptions of you. So stand up straight, make good eye contact, smile, shake hands firmly, and stop fidgeting! Most of these instructions sound simple, but you would be surprised when I'm working with clients or doing a seminar how many people really struggle with body language, because oftentimes the way you stand or fidget is a habit that can be hard to break. So don't be too hard on yourself if it takes you a while. Just do your best and take it one day at a time.

Coaching Exercise 3

1. The next time you are in a meeting or attend an event, observe other people's body language and make a mental note—it will help you become more aware of your own.

2. Honestly evaluate each area detailed in this chapter. Where are your strengths? *If you're not sure, ask someone whom you trust to evaluate you in this area.*

3. Where are your opportunities for improvement?

4. What actions will you specifically take to improve? List three things you can do.

    a.

    b.

    c.

CHAPTER 4

Ways to Boost Your
Public Speaking Confidence

"Enthusiasm is one of the most powerful engines of success. When you do a thing, do it with all your might. Put your whole soul into it. Stamp it with your own personality. Be active, be energetic, be enthusiastic and faithful, and you will accomplish your object. Nothing great was ever achieved without enthusiasm."

—Ralph Waldo Emerson

No one can give you confidence; it has to come from within. In one area in particular, it is essential to have confidence—public speaking. The average person is filled with dread when you put them in front of a podium, at the front of a boardroom, or in a room full of people. **To be successful you can't be average! You have to master public speaking and learn how to leverage it to promote yourself, your business, and your brand.** Although each of us has the ability to enunciate words to form speech, that does not mean that all of us possess the ability to communicate effectively. In this chapter I share seven easy ways to boost your public speaking confidence.

1. Practice, practice, practice!

Like anything in life, the more you do something, the more confident you get. Public speaking is no different. If you don't have any speaking engagements or presentations lined up, then speak in front of friends, join a club, or even speak in front of the mirror. No excuses—just do it!

2. Get feedback and act on it.

When you do have the opportunity to speak in front of other people, ask them for feedback and suggestions for improvement. You may not like what they have to say, but it will make you a better speaker. Why? Because you are not speaking for yourself, but for your audience, so listen attentively to what they have to say.

3. Build on your strengths.

As an executive speech coach, one thing I find fascinating is that people always focus on their weaknesses and not on their strengths. You will build on whatever you focus on—so it stands to reason that if you focus on your strengths, you will develop them even further and be more successful as a result.

4. Silence your inner critic.

We all have that voice inside us that says, *You're going to make a fool of yourself*, or, *Oh God, they're all staring at me and I don't know what to say!* The difference between an average public speaker and a great one is that the former listens to their inner critic, and the latter talks back to their inner critic and says, *Shut the hell up, it's my turn to speak!*

"If there's only one thing you take out of this book, it needs to be this: You must believe in yourself at all times. Why? If you don't believe in yourself, your audience will see right through you."

---

5. Look the part.

This sounds self-evident, but particularly for women, it's a big one. For men it's often simple; just put on a good suit that fits well. For a woman it can be more complicated. You need to strike a balance between professional, stylish, and appropriate. Above all, your appearance needs to project credibility. Remember that public speaking is visual by its very nature, so how you present yourself is essential to your success.

6. Take a course.

When you stop learning, you die inside. Take self-development courses; attend webinars and read books and ebooks on a whole range of subjects on a regular basis. Hire a coach in an area of concern. If you don't have the time, then make the time. Invest in yourself—it's worth it!

7. Believe in yourself.

If there's only one thing you take out of this book, it needs to be this: You must believe in yourself at all times. Why? If you don't believe in yourself, your audience will see right through you.

Confidence is at the heart of every great human achievement. When it comes to public speaking, you have to decide who you are. Are you an average person who is going to be intimidated by public speaking and muddle your way through life without this essential skill? Or are you an entrepreneurial superstar, with the ability to communicate your message to the world? I know which one I am!

Coaching Exercise 4

1. This is one of the most important chapters in the book—don't skim or skip it if you need to go back and read it again (seriously)!

2. In your own professional life, where do you have the opportunity to practice public speaking?

3. Whom can you ask to give you feedback on your speaking?

4. What three things does your inner critic say to you?

    a.

    b.

    c.

5. Where can you find one-on-one coaching or group training on public speaking in your company or in your city?

CHAPTER 5

The 7 Pillars of High-Impact Speaking

"Without knowing the force of words, it is impossible to know men."

—Confucius

Boring people is easy. *Dazzling* people is difficult. You need to be *amazing* if you're going to succeed. Good just doesn't cut it anymore. Why? Because there's too much competition out there. This chapter is about giving you tips to take your public speaking and presentation skills to even greater heights. Again, you need to be selective and continue striving for excellence in your communication skills. In some circumstances, such as a conference keynote address, where you're speaking to thousands of people—it's your reputation (and sometimes your job, too) on the line. You can't afford to let your pride get in the way. So use these tips as a starting place and see how you can incorporate them into your next major speech or presentation. Here are seven ways to dazzle your audience.

1. Write killer content.

Great speeches begin with great writing. This always surprises my clients. The last thing many people think of when you talk about public speaking or presentation skills is good writing. At the soul of both speaking and writing is the ability to communicate your thoughts and emotions with clarity and power. That's at the heart of what I help my clients do. With these tips, you will be better able to do that yourself. Having said that, remember to have a combination of written talking points (that you memorize, not read!) and spontaneous thoughts—all well-structured together.

"At the soul of both speaking and writing is the ability to communicate your thoughts and emotions with clarity and power."

2. Use props or people.

You know the old adage, "Don't tell me, show me." Well, that's what I'm talking about here. So don't be afraid to use props that are relevant to your presentation, integrate video into your presentation, or even have people come up and support your message. You could bring people up to the stage (if appropriate) to demonstrate something or give their perspective or share their story. That's something I do a lot in my keynotes and workshops—it's very powerful.

3. Dress to stand out.

About eight times out of ten, I see people on stage wear the standard boring black suit. Why would you do that, when there are so many beautiful colors in the universe? Again, you need to comfortable in the spotlight to begin with, and that's usually the problem. Also this principle does not apply when you're doing a high-level boardroom presentation where you may want to blend in more. So use common sense, too.

4. Act out.

Use your entire body to describe what you're trying to say. I spend hours working on body language with my clients. It's a huge part of any speakers' repertoire, and something that people often underutilize. Imagine that you're an actor on stage at your local theatre—how would you act out what you're trying to say?

5. Use your voice.

A flat, monotone voice is so dull. **Imagine that your voice is a landscape—you want mountains and valleys. That way you'll make your audience's journey more interesting.** So learn to really use your voice—raise and lower the volume—speed it up and slow it down. Remember, you should easily be heard from the back of the room. Plus, always practice with the microphone if you're going to be using one on the day of your speaking event. I take my clients through exercises with all types of microphones—from lapel to handheld and headset to no microphone at all.

"Ultimately, public speaking is a transformative art. Your words can change someone's life for the better by giving them useful information, inspiring them to take action, or giving them a new perspective on an issue."

6. Respond to your audience.

It's important that throughout your presentation or keynote, you take cues from your audience. This takes attention and experience, but start with the basics. The next time you are presenting to an audience, ask yourself: How do they look? Interested and engaged or bored? Are they asking questions? Be flexible and respond to their needs. One of the best compliments I ever received for my speaking came from another presenter at the same conference as me, when she said, "I was running my workshop in the room next to yours—we kept hearing applause and laughter. What were you guys doing?" I felt so good after she said that.

7. End BIG.

You want to end with something that will be both powerful and memorable. For example, you could try an emotionally charged personal story, or a bold call to take action. Something to remember! Ultimately, public speaking is a transformative art. Your words can change someone's life for the better by giving them useful information, inspiring them to take action, or giving them a new perspective on an issue.

We've gone through seven ways to make a more commanding impression, the next time you have a presentation to give or are delivering a keynote at a conference. The key is to take one idea and implement it each time you take the stage (or the front of the boardroom). You can become a much more powerful speaker, with a lot of hard work and a little help from me.

Coaching Exercise 5

1. What can you do to improve your writing skills?

2. Evaluate your current wardrobe. Do most of your professional outfits blend in or stand out?

3. Make an audio recording of yourself on your smartphone or laptop. Is your voice flat and dull or lively and exciting?

4. What props can you bring to your next presentation or keynote?

PART TWO:

COACHING MOMENTS

CHAPTER 6

Ways to Overcome Your Own Fear and Self-Doubt

"If you are distressed by anything external, the pain is not due to the thing itself, but to your estimate of it; and this you have the power to revoke at any moment."

—Marcus Aurelius

What's stopping you from achieving your goals and dreams? You have the tools and the talent, but something is holding you back. When businesses fail, people often blame external factors such as the economy, lack of cash flow, or anything other than themselves. Of course, these factors are important. But why is it that some businesses succeed while others fail—in the same economy, even the same industry? It's simple—it's the people running the businesses who are different.

Here are some tips that you will help you overcome your biggest obstacle—yourself.

Visualize success.

You must have a clear vision for your business, career, and life. For example, if it's your business you're working on, then your business model and ultimately your business plan will be based on your vision. If you stumbled into your business, like so many people do, there is still time to refine and focus your vision.

Surround yourself with positive people.

This is something I come back to again and again in my mind. We all have those days when everything seems to go wrong, and it's so hard to keep pushing forward. That's when you need to turn to your family and friends and absorb their encouragement and positive energy.

Seek expert advice.

If you have a mental block, or if you need to solve a problem or develop a specific area of your business, then get help. I have a business coach in one key area of my business. I'm actually surprised by how many entrepreneurs feel they know everything and can solve every problem alone. That's just ridiculous! Reach out and get an expert to help you.

"So rip out the fear and self-doubt that have been plaguing your dreams and allow faith and positive energy to propel you toward your true destiny."

Stop being afraid.

Are you scared of failure, success, or something else? Regardless of what it is, get over it! Fear holds you back; it stops you from taking risks and seeing new opportunities. I know it's easier said than done, but if I can do it, then so can you.

Believe in your vision.

We come full circle with this one. You have a vision, so now you have to believe in it with every ounce of your being.

Pour your heart and soul into it. Don't allow doubt to enter your mind for even a moment.

Recently I've had so many people ask me what is the secret to my success. So listen up, here it is—*a change in mind-set.* After years of self-doubt and fear, I finally believe in myself and the power of my dreams. You have what it takes, but now you need to take that leap of faith and believe that you have the power to realize your dreams. So rip out the fear and self-doubt that have been plaguing your dreams and allow faith and positive energy to propel you toward your true destiny.

Coaching Exercise 6

1. Pick a real-life situation coming up where you have to speak and visualize yourself going through it and doing a great job. How did it feel?

2. List three positive people whom you want to spend more time with and why.

   a.

   b.

   c.

3. What kind of experts do you need to work with?

4. What are you really afraid of when it comes to public speaking? There is no right or wrong answer here.

Difficult Situations and Delivering Bad News

"What we think or what we know or what we believe is, in the end, of little consequence. The only consequence is what we do."

—John Ruskin

"I am sorry." Those three little words can bring closure to the most difficult situation and rescue almost any business relationship from ruin. The ability to apologize or deliver bad news is a dying art in today's hectic world. We avoid it, rush it, and overcomplicate it. It should be sincere, simple, and non-technical.

This chapter is written with communications and public relations professionals in mind, who often have to deal with difficult situations and deliver bad news in the spotlight.

Here are some tips to make it easier and more effective.

Remember, it's not about you.

There will be times when you need to apologize or deliver bad news, even when you don't think you've done anything wrong or the news should not come from you. The married folks among us can attest to this! Swallow your pride and apologize anyway. Perhaps you or your organization unintentionally offended a particular individual or group. Whatever the reason—what matters is the listeners' perception of the situation, not your own. Try to see things from their perspective when you speak.

Use simple language.

Sometimes the simplest language is also the most powerful. "I love you" is a great example of this. When crafting your apology or statement, either in writing or in person, remember that all the other person really wants to hear is "I am sorry" or "I apologize." Information should be delivered clearly with no technical jargon.

Delete the BUT.

If you say, "I'm sorry, *but* I don't think I did anything wrong," or "I'm sorry, *but* this news isn't coming from me..." the qualifier negates any good you are trying to do. Another mistake that often rears its head is, "I think you're overreacting, but I'm sorry anyway." Again, try to imagine how it will sound to the listener.

"There will be times when you need to apologize or deliver bad news, even when you don't think you've done anything wrong or the news should not come from you."

Work out the details.

The only way to successfully augment an apology or bad news is with a real reason and information—laid out with unnecessary blame or accusation. For example, say, "I'm sorry for interrupting you during the presentation," or "I know I upset you yesterday; I'm sorry." It shows that you have reflected on the situation and appreciate how the other person feels. (Even if you don't think you've done anything wrong, it still may be your responsibility to deliver the news or apologize.)

Slow down.

If you're apologizing or delivering the bad news in person or over the phone (as I hope you are, rather than texting or e-mailing first), slow down when you say the words. Anything said slowly shows more thought and sincerity. Try it: Say anything slowly and you'll see the difference it makes.

Don't text it or tweet it.

As I mentioned in the previous point, some things are private, and they need to remain that way. The best way to deliver bad news or get through a difficult situation is either in person or over the phone—they need to hear your voice. The next best way is in an e-mail or snail-mail card (depending on your preference). Please don't tweet your apology or news for the entire world to see, or send a cursory text message. A person reading from a statement is always better than a statement delivered for the news anchor to read—you will be able to add feeling and sincerity to the words.

Remember that it takes grace and tact to apologize or deliver difficult news.

The ability to apologize and deliver bad news needs to be part of any successful person's communications arsenal. Without it, your relationships will suffer, but with it, they will stand the test of time.

Coaching Exercise 7

1. Is there a situation in your professional or personal life where you need to deliver bad news or speak through a difficult situation?

2. What do you need to communicate in this situation?

3. What would the consequences be if you didn't communicate this?

4. When has an organization used technology to communicate something when it was better done in person?

CHAPTER 8

Speaking to Stand Up for Yourself

"It takes two to speak the truth—one to speak, and another to hear."

—Henry David Thoreau

Usually in my keynotes I talk about breaking down boundaries to improve communication. But in some situations it's important to stand your ground and learn to say no. This chapter is more about general communication skills than public speaking, but it's important enough that I wanted to include it anyway. There are many reasons why people find it hard to say no—they don't want to upset anyone, they want everyone to like them, they want to avoid confrontation, or they don't want to lose someone's business. Recently I had to say no to a client. It was a difficult decision for me, because I'm the sort of person (perhaps like you) who bends over backward for my customers, and I usually do anything within my power to make them happy. But in this situation I was beginning to feel like I was being taken advantage of, so after a lot of soul searching I decided to say *no*. I salvaged the relationship, and everything worked out. The time I spent reflecting on that situation inspired this chapter.

Here are some situations where it would be beneficial for you to say no or stand up for yourself.

You feel uncomfortable.

You're in a meeting with a colleague, and he shares a derogatory or sexual comment or joke and you suddenly feel uncomfortable. (This has happened to me more than once, I can tell you!) Now it could be something innocent or it could be that they are just being a big bully. Yes, there are bullies in the business world, too. Most people in this situation would say nothing. *Wrong!* People will respect you more, and you will respect yourself more, if you do say something—draw clear boundaries and tell the other person how you feel: "I don't need to hear any more jokes or comments like that. I hope you understand." If the behavior doesn't stop, tell someone you report to or someone in Human Resources—I would even put it in writing. Handle it in a calm and respectful manner so it reflects well on your professionalism.

You are procrastinating to start a project.

Learning to say no is a powerful tool to help you overcome procrastination. Perhaps you've been putting off a particular project again and again, because it just doesn't interest you. So why did you say yes in the first place? I can't answer that question—but it's something for you to think about. You also need to reconcile yourself with the fact that you have to just get on with it, finish what you committed to do, and next time say no to start with. Remember that at the root of procrastination is often a lack of self-confidence—so if you move forward and take action, you will working to build the confidence that you lack.

You are underestimating your worth.

So many people underestimate the value of their time. If you set a flat fee for a project and have estimated a specific amount of time and now it's gone way, way over that allotment, it may be time to sit down with your client and explain the situation. If they keep making changes to the initial project specifications and you keep putting in the time for a flat fee, eventually you'll be earning little more than minimum wage, when you work it out hourly. It's time to say no, politely of course. This conversation must happen either in person or over the phone—not in an e-mail or text message! Then next time estimate a realistic amount of time.

"People will respect you more, and you will respect yourself more, if you do say something—draw clear boundaries and tell the other person how you feel."

You are overworked and overstressed.

You've heard the expression, "If you want something done, give it to someone who's busy." Well, I agree with that to a point—but if you're so busy that your life is out of balance, and you don't have the time to get anything done, then you need to say no to something. Something has to give so you can reestablish your equilibrium.

Learning how to say this simple two-letter word—*no*—will slowly help you evolve into a more successful person because you will procrastinate less, manage your time better, quote more realistic fees (and, as a result, make more profit), and establish boundaries with your colleagues. So pick one situation today where you need to take charge, then speak up and stand up for yourself.

Coaching Exercise 8

1. Think about an upcoming project or situation where you need to speak up to create a boundary. Go through it in your mind and write down what you want to say.

2. When is the last time another person's comments or questions derailed you when you were speaking? What could you have done differently?

CHAPTER 9

When to Use PowerPoint (and When Not To!)

"Believe nothing. No matter where you read it, or who said it, even if I have said it, unless it agrees with your own reason and your own common sense."

—Buddha

Most businesspeople learn how to use PowerPoint before they learn anything about public speaking. That seems strange to me, but as is the case in our society—the technology comes first. In fact, most jobs require at least a rudimentary knowledge of the program. I was surprised recently to learn that it's taught in elementary schools now. Wow, how times have changed—I'm getting old! So, is it still relevant? Yes, absolutely, even after all these years PowerPoint is still the industry leader. But this chapter is concerned more with giving you some guidelines so you know *when* to use PowerPoint (or any presentation technology or app), and more importantly, when not to. Some good applications for PowerPoint include the following.

Technical presentations

Over the years I've worked with architects, engineers, and information technology professionals, all of whom routinely have to give highly technical presentations that need a program like PowerPoint. So if you have data, graphs, charts, diagrams, etc., then, of course, use it! But don't let the technical side of your presentation bog you down in jargon and disconnect you from your audience.

Training/leading workshops and seminars

For training of any kind to be effective, you must organize your thoughts and structure your content in a logical manner. One of the best ways to do that is to use PowerPoint. You can even brainstorm right into the outline mode, and work from there. Many times that's what I do.

> *"Remember that any presentation technology can act like a barrier between you and your audience."*

Longer keynotes

Many of my clients just can't live without a memory aid such as notes, note cards, etc., for their longer speeches. Another great memory aid is PowerPoint. Keep the presentation concise and focused for best results. Remember, if your presentation is long and crazy—that's how you're going to sound! Don't say I didn't warn you. One client had ninety slides for a forty-five-minute presentation—that's way too many. Edit, edit, edit.

Sales presentations

The classic sales presentation needs PowerPoint—to outline purchase options, packages, benefits, testimonials, etc. For that you're going to need a clean, professional, and visually dynamic presentation. Remember to give your listeners the relevant details printed out, too.

Here are some not-so-good applications.

High-impact keynotes

If you're doing a town hall meeting or a speech for the board of trade, do *not* use PowerPoint if you can help it. You're just going to bore people to death—trust me on this one! I have been there in the audience, cringing for my client (who didn't listen to me) and bored out of my mind.

I remember one keynote in particular—by a business-woman speaking at an all-day conference I was attending. She was one of the main keynote speakers of the day, and of course I was looking forward to hearing what she had to say. She had forty-five minutes for her keynote, which is typical. At the beginning of her speech she said that she was going to make twelve points and then her PowerPoint came on. Unfortunately her speech took much longer than expected, and she realized she was only going to get to six points. As she started trying to skip slides with her presentation remote, she got frazzled and went forward, then backward haphazardly. Her PowerPoint began to distract her and made her even more nervous than she had been before. She made a number of mistakes that day (not a client of mine!), including not practicing her entire keynote with the PowerPoint to see the timing. The one that stood out to me was how disorganized it looked—it would have been easier to salvage the organization and timing if she hadn't been using any presentation technology.

Team engagement

When you want to inspire and uplift, I don't recommend you use PowerPoint. Remember that any presentation technology can act like a barrier between you and your audience. This is particularly true of a leader speaking to his/her employees or team members. It should be just be you and your voice.

Small group meeting

Sometimes when your setting is more intimate—a small meeting or more intimate event, PowerPoint is not the best way to go. Instead, use this opportunity to really get to know the people listening to you—engage more, listen more, and talk less.

There are so many more tips I could give you on Power-Point, but these will suffice as a good beginning. Remember also that presentation technology can be very polarizing—some people switch off right away when they see a projector come on, while other people embrace it and look forward to it. I'm somewhere in between. So be more selective when using it and you will see an immediate improvement in your presentation skills.

Coaching Exercise 9

1. In the last few presentations you've done, did you use PowerPoint? How many times?

2. Think back. Did it really help improve your presentation? Why or why not?

3. Do you use PowerPoint as it is meant to be used or as a crutch?

4. Go through the slides of an upcoming presentation and edit it for clarity and consistency.

CHAPTER 10

Integrating Public Speaking into Your Strategic Plan

"The secret of getting ahead is getting started. The secret of getting started is breaking your complex, overwhelming tasks into small, manageable tasks, and then starting on the first one."

—Mark Twain

Public speaking should be an integral part of your business plan, marketing strategy, or even career plan. You must be able to conceptualize what you want to achieve and how you're going to achieve it, then put public speaking or presentations in the mix. But I'm getting ahead of myself—let's get started and you'll see what I mean.

Add it to your plan.

I'm always surprised when I work with entrepreneurs and business owners at how many of them don't have written marketing plans or even up-to-date business plans with a marketing component. I don't understand that at all. Every business or project—small or large—should have such a document, and it should be revised and reevaluated on a regular basis according to results achieved. Public speaking in all its forms—keynotes, seminars, workshops, webinars, boardroom presentations, etc.—should be integrated into your document. *If you're not sure how to get started with your plan, go to my recommended reading list at the back of the book and look for Guy Kawasaki's book—he has a great chapter on planning.*

Create signature keynotes or content.

I could probably write a whole chapter just on creating signature keynotes, but for now, suffice it to say that you need to have two to three good speeches ready to go at any given time. They should be well written and organized, but still flexible enough to change at the drop of a hat, given the audience and type of event. You should also take into consideration the purpose of the event, so don't do a keynote meant to sell your products and services at a high school event meant to educate the students.

Send an e-mail newsletter.

Send your customers, colleagues, or stakeholders an opt-in e-newsletter or a snail-mail letter, or both. Make sure you mention upcoming events, presentations, educational opportunities, speaking engagements, etc. In terms of frequency, you need to strike a balance. Don't send it so often that you irritate them, but not so infrequently that they forget who you are. Don't overwhelm them with information and special offers, either—keep it simple. Two to three points is enough, including a personal introduction. You should sound as if you are writing to a friend,

not a mass mailing list. Most businesses implement this step and stop there, thinking their job is done. Actually, this is just the beginning.

Communicate and connect through social media.

The next step is to use social media to keep in touch with your clients, colleagues, and stakeholders. Become their contact and follow their status updates, commenting occasionally. Actively engage them in conversation from time to time. Comment on their posts or share interesting content with your circle of friends.

The key elements here are *engagement* and *reciprocity*. Again, remember to promote upcoming speaking opportunities, webinars, etc. Some social media platforms are particularly effective when you use photos and video because public speaking is such a visual medium. Remember to use real language and be authentic and fun in your communications—people appreciate that. You can also upload your presentation slides to your profile by connecting various applications to your profile.

Blog about it.

Write a blog post about a speech you're going to give or have already given. Talk about what it meant to you and/or your business. If you don't write well or don't have the time to write—hire someone who does! Seriously, it's worth it. Remember to promote your blog post by posting links to your social media platforms, too.

Communicate in person and by word of mouth.

The most fundamental of all forms of communication is also the most powerful—person-to-person contact, such as picking up the phone to talk to someone. The less technology is involved, the more powerful your message will be. I did this recently with a client I hadn't heard from in the longest time, only to find that he had been in a serious car accident. He was grateful for the call and appreciated having someone to talk to. I made a note on his file to follow up with him again in a month. Reach out to one of your customers today by picking up the phone. Don't just reach out to tell them about an upcoming speech or presentation—do it because it's the right thing to do, and then if it comes up in the conversation (which it probably will), great!

Use snail mail.

Send a handwritten note to tell them about an upcoming event or seminar or even just to say hello. In our electronic age, the fact that you made the effort to write something meaningful to someone will make you stand out from the crowd. It will look even more professional if you have personalized stationery or note cards with your initials or logo on them. This is a small investment, considering the impact it makes.

"The most fundamental of all forms of communication is also the most powerful—person-to-person contact, such as picking up the phone to talk to someone. The less technology is involved, the more powerful your message will be."

Add it to your e-mail signature.

You can add extra information about upcoming events to your e-mail signature if it is timely and appropriate. Remember not to make your signature too long—people hate that—but still it's a great promotion tool, so why not use it?

Ultimately you need to show everyone that you genuinely care about them as people first. **There are so many ways that you can integrate public speaking into your career, business, or marketing plan. Use every means at your disposal to get the word out about your speaking so it promotes you, your project, and your business.** It's a win-win because you want to reach the people who genuinely need to hear your message— but if you don't tell anyone, then how will they know?

Coaching Exercise 10

1. Do you currently have a personal development plan, business plan, or marketing plan?

2. If your answer was no, sit down and use the space below to start creating a one- or two-page document that outlines your goals and how you can integrate public speaking to achieve them.

3. If your answer was yes, sit down and figure out how to integrate public speaking with your current goals—in both cases, remember to be selective!

4. What other ways can you think of to publicize or promote your speaking?

PART THREE

PUBLIC SPEAKING IN REAL LIFE

CHAPTER 11

Fundamentals of a Successful Sales Pitch

"It is the long history of humankind (and animal kind, too) that those who learned to collaborate and improvise most effectively have prevailed."

—Charles Darwin

Almost everyone will, at some point in their professional life, have to give a persuasive presentation of some kind in a boardroom setting. Anytime you want to persuade people to see things your way and buy in to a concept or product, you're selling. *Sales* is not a bad word—but many people think of it that way. You are an ambassador for your company or organization whenever you stand up to speak— whether it's at a meeting in a boardroom or on stage at a conference. So here are some tips to make the best of it!

Research, plan ahead, and know your numbers.

Before you step foot in that boardroom, you must know as much as you can about the people who are going to be there with you. Research the company and the stakeholders through the Internet and social media. If you already know them, then think about what motivates them to be there for this specific presentation and how you can appeal to that. You also need to know your numbers—inside and out.

"You are an ambassador for your company or organization whenever you stand up to speak—whether it's at a meeting in a boardroom or on stage at a conference."

Believe in yourself.

This is essential. You must believe in your own ability and speak with confidence. Hopefully reading this book and implementing my suggestions will have helped you along the way. If you're presenting to the executive suite, then they will see right through any pretenses, so you have to be authentic, be strong, and show no fear.

Believe in your product or idea.

The greatest asset you have when you try to persuade someone of your perspective is your own faith in the product or idea. When I'm coaching my clients or working with teams, I often find that this component is missing, especially if it's "just a job" and they "have to make this presentation." You must believe in the product, service, or idea you are trying to sell, or don't do it! If you don't believe in it, don't sell it—it's that simple.

Believe in your team.

More and more, I see team presentations, especially in service-based industries such as the legal field or advertising. You must have faith in your fellow presenters. Don't interrupt them. Don't correct them. Don't undermine them—intentionally or unintentionally. Be a true team player and let them shine just as brightly as you do.

> *"If you're presenting to the executive suite, then they will see right through any pretenses, so you have to be authentic, be strong, and show no fear."*

Be flexible.

Be open to questions and comments from your listeners. Don't let them get you flustered or allow them to derail what you're trying to say. Another option is to say that you'll take questions at the end of the presentation—that's up to you. If you don't know the answer to a question, either ask a colleague to jump in, or if you're on your own, tell the person you'll find out the answer and get back to them.

Be friendly.

The most effective sales presentations take place when you relax and make it fun. I know that's hard to do when you have a lot on the line and it's do or die. But you must try to be the fun, happy, and friendly person that you are in real life and not let the context make you an uptight mess (which is what I often see, unfortunately).

Be authentic.

Don't try to be like someone else—just be yourself. **It's important to be authentic in all your communications and let people see the real you—not some façade that you think they want you to be.** So allow yourself to be vulnerable and emotional if the mood strikes you, as long as it doesn't undermine your credibility and make you say something inappropriate. Another key is to draw from your own personal experiences to make your points more powerful.

Repeat, wrap up, and respond.

Repeat important points in any sales presentation again near the end, and then wrap it up. Don't ramble on like a crazy person. Stop talking and start listening—that's when the magic happens! Even if you don't agree with what someone has to say, don't interrupt them, let them finish, then think of an intelligent response.

One of my favorite business books on the art of persuasion is by Arlene Dickinson—I've listed it in the recommended reading section at the back of this book. It is a great read—worth the time. Be responsive to what people have to say and genuinely try to see things from their perspective—it will help when you're negotiating with them. Ultimately you want your sales pitch to result in a win-win for everyone concerned, so you need to make sure you have addressed their concerns, objections, and needs. This isn't an episode of a reality television show where people pitch in for two to three minutes; in real life it could take a few minutes or it could take an hour—make sure you have put aside enough time, and good luck!

Coaching Exercise 11

1. Make an written outline for a sales pitch or presentation you need to give in the next six months. Which stakeholders will be there? What do you know about them?

2. Will you be doing a solo pitch or a team presentation? Do you have faith in your team members? Do you need to take some training together?

3. What are the most important points you need to make to achieve your objective?

CHAPTER 12

Speaking at an Awards Gala:
How to Give a Great Acceptance Speech

"If people knew how hard I had to work to gain my mastery, it wouldn't seem wonderful at all."

—Michelangelo

Accepting an award can be one of the most gratifying moments in a persons' career. Giving an acceptance speech under tremendous emotional pressure and in front of hundreds of people can be a nerve-racking experience, leaving the best of us tongue-tied. You may even have a family or staff member video-tape it on their phone to upload to the Internet later— so you may have an even much larger audience than who's in the room with you. Are you ready? Here are five tips to help you make the best impression at the podium.

1. Dress your best.

You get nominated for an award through the local chamber or business association—what's the first thing you do? Go shopping for something new to wear, of course! For most award ceremonies you want to look glamorous, but still professional. Remember, you'll want to use photos of the awards on future marketing materials, so don't wear anything too revealing or too crazy. You also want to stand out, so consider wearing a color that complements your skin tone instead of boring old black.

2.   Speak from the heart.

Don't just tell them how you feel; *show* them how you feel. If you're overwhelmed, take a moment, it will add to the drama of the speech. If you want to scream with excitement, that's great, too! Tell them a personal story or share some of the sacrifices you have had to make to reach this point in your life. Make it personal and real for your audience.

3.   Watch your filler words.

When you're nervous, one of the first things to happen is...um, err, ah. You know what I'm talking about, those ugly filler words that say nothing and take away from your credibility. Working on your pace and breathing will help control the onslaught of filler words. It's not an overnight process, so practice this well in advance.

"Tell them a personal story or share some of the sacrifices you have had to make to reach this point in your life. Make it personal and real for your audience."

---

4.   Be prepared, but not too prepared.

You know you've been nominated, so now the work begins. Research the award and the other nominees. Invite friends and family to the awards gala so you have friendly faces to look at when you get to the podium. Remember to thank people and be gracious, but please don't pull out a list!

Great speeches are a balance of good writing and spontaneous bursts of brilliance.

5. Be quirky.

This is one you probably haven't heard before. People try too hard to be funny and usually bomb as a result. Instead, why not be quirky? For example, you could thank someone unexpected, like a teacher from your school days or your psychiatrist! It will make your speech more interesting and probably get more laughs than you think.

Remember, just the fact that you've been nominated means that people have noticed your hard work and accomplishments. It is an honor just to be nominated—that's not just something people say, it's true! Share the good news of your award nomination and/or win in your bio, on your website, on your social media profiles, and anywhere else you can think of. That way your accomplishments will live on forever.

Coaching Exercise 12

1. Think of an award in your field, maybe an internal award through your organization or an external one through the local chamber of commerce. Put together a plan to apply for it.

2. Now imagine the time has come to accept this award. Write your acceptance speech. Keep it tight and snappy.

3. Visualize yourself accepting the award. How does it feel?

4. Practice actually giving the speech—in front of the mirror or to a friend or your public speaking coach.

CHAPTER 13

Speaking on TV:
Do's and Don'ts of Media Appearances

"Seeing's believing, but feeling's the truth."

—Thomas Fuller, M.D.

One day you get the call—a television news station wants to do an interview with you. You are excited and terrified at the same time, because this is your first television interview. You should be very proud. I've been there, and it's an awesome feeling! For some people in the public eye, being in the media is a regular occurrence and it can either help or hinder their career. Here are some tips so you can maximize this opportunity.

Be prepared.

Perhaps they are calling you because you have positioned yourself as an expert, or because you have a compelling story to share. Either way, be prepared for the types of questions they might ask you. If you have the time, study the style of the journalist who will interview you or even the program itself. Will it be live or recorded? Will they come to you, or will you go to their studio? Will you get to review the questions ahead of time? Will you be a part of a panel? How long will you have to speak?

Dress the part.

This is obvious, I know, and I've mentioned it in previous chapters, too, but I still see coaches, consultants, and other businesspeople on television looking like they just woke up and put on the first thing they could find! If they don't do your hair and makeup (and many don't have the budget for it), then you do it and make sure it's good. Don't go *au naturel*. Makeup is essential on television—trust me, it makes a big difference on camera.

Stay calm.

Breathe in, breathe out, and repeat. I can promise you that you are going to be stressed out by the experience. If it's your first time on TV, you will find all the different lights, cameras, and microphones distracting—try to stay focused on your message. I remember my first time—I felt like the bright lights were burning into my skin.

Be authentic.

I always tell my clients to be authentic. Never try to impress people. Just be yourself. Once you start worrying about what other people think of you, you lose your focus and it undermines your confidence. Being authentic and relaxed will also help you communicate more clearly.

Smile.

Have you ever noticed how elected officials smile on camera? If it's appropriate to your message—smile. It's surprisingly hard to do when you're new to media interviews because there's so much going on. But if you want to come across as the friendly, warm, compassionate person that you are (again we're being authentic, so don't pretend to be someone you're not), you need to smile.

> *"Never try to impress people. Just be yourself. Once you start worrying about what other people think of you, you lose your focus and it undermines your confidence. Being authentic and relaxed will also help you communicate more clearly."*

Make good eye contact.

Your eyes need to make contact with the reporter interviewing you (unless they tell you otherwise). Don't dart your eyes around the room or look up and down. Good eye contact shows strength of character and trust.

Be confident.

Confidence ties all the above points together. As I've said in previous chapters, it has to come from within. Your confidence has to shine through your eyes, your smile, and of course your words. Remember that if it's a good interview, they might call you again!

Being interviewed on television is just another form of public speaking. You have an audience (maybe even bigger than you think), and you need to stay on message and use your body language to make a first-rate impression. **Above all, allow yourself to feel good about your accomplishments and enjoy your moment in the spotlight.**

Coaching Exercise 13

1. When was the last time you were interviewed on TV? How did it go? Did you say what you planned or did you get frazzled and talk nonsense?

2. If you haven't been on TV before, what have you done or achieved recently that is newsworthy? Write a simple press release and send it out to local TV stations—you can easily get the contact information through their websites.

3. Many of these principles also apply to speaking on video. Ask a friend or colleague to video-tape you speaking and then analyze yourself. It's very different from what you think you look like!

CHAPTER 14

Speaking at Weddings and Special Occasions: How to Give a Great Special Toast

"Rules for Happiness:
something to do,
someone to love,
something to hope for."
—Immanuel Kant

There are many reasons people get together throughout the year, from holidays (like Hanukkah, Christmas, New Year's, Diwali, etc.) to family dinners, from weddings to corporate parties. Regardless of what the special occasion is, you should be able to give a great toast or mini-speech that will inspire in your audience a sense of joy and togetherness. Very few people know this about me, but one of my previous jobs was as a catering sales manager and wedding planner at a prestigious Vancouver wedding venue. It was one of the most stressful years of my life. But one thing I can tell you, I saw a lot of special occasion toasts and speeches. Unlike many of the other events covered in this book that talk about business-type events, where it's mostly colleagues and clients in the audience, at this type of event you're talking to the people with the longest memories, your family and friends. These people won't let you live down anything—so it's important that you get it right! I've also seen people who would be more confident in a business situation become uncomfortable when they have to speak from a more personal place—so take that into consideration, too, and don't be too hard on yourself.

Here are some tips to make your toast special for any occasion.

Don't drink and speak.

Now I know that during a special occasion, people drink, and that's fine. What I'm saying is, don't get inebriated *and then speak*—you're going to sound like an idiot, slur your speech, and make a fool of yourself! Speaking sober is my recommendation—drink after, not before.

Share a personal story.

Nothing touches people more than a personal story or experience shared. Keep it short, though; don't ramble on. There is an art to storytelling, and that's something I always work on with my clients.

Don't tell an Internet joke.

Unless you have amazing comedic timing, telling an Internet joke is never a good idea. If you tell your personal story right, you will be able to infuse it with natural humor and get people laughing anyway.

Use the full potential of your voice.

When you give a toast, you typically raise your glass, right? Well, you should do the same thing with your voice—use its full potential and make it as varied as possible. This is a tough one for many people and something I work hard on with my executive speech coaching clients. Try your best — your audience will appreciate it.

Use *big* body language and gestures.

A toast is a grand gesture that should fill the room with warm, positive energy that enthrals your colleagues, friends, and family. That's not going to happen if you are slouching with a frown on your face. So stand up straight, smile, and use big arm and hand gestures to really liven things up.

"A toast is a grand gesture that should fill the room with warm, positive energy that enthrals your colleagues, friends, and family."

Practice on your family or coworkers.

It's always a good idea to write down what you're going to say (don't read it, though—memorize it), and practice on people you trust and get their honest opinion.

We have just gone through six keys to giving a great special occasion toast. Now put them to good use. Remember, sometimes a special occasion toast can be even more important than a business presentation because all your family and friends are there to hear you (no pressure!) and you won't want to disappoint them. So take your time to plan and practice so you will make it memorable and meaningful to everyone.

Coaching Exercise 14

1. In the next twelve months, will you have the opportunity or be required to make a toast or special occasion speech?

2. If so, what type of event is it?

3. How long will you have to speak?

4. How many people will be there?

5. Start writing down an outline and get as much practice as you can!

CHAPTER 15

Impromptu Speaking at Events: Networking Do's and Don'ts

"It is one of the beautiful compensations of this life that no man can sincerely try to help another without helping himself."

—Ralph Waldo Emerson

As I write this chapter, I'm getting ready to go to a networking event. I try to limit myself to two to three a month; otherwise it can be a little overwhelming for my already busy schedule. **Why is a public speaking and presentation skills coach talking about networking? Because networking is front-line, face-to-face communication, that you must master.** You have mere seconds to make a powerful first impression or they'll switch off and you've lost them forever. So here's my list of do's and don'ts for networking.

Do remember that quality is more important than quantity.

Networking is about building relationships, not getting as many business cards as possible. It's better to make one or two meaningful connections at an event than leave with a pocket full of business cards of people you barely remember.

Don't hit me over the head with your business card.

This is a big pet peeve of mine. People always pull out their business card right away—I think the polite thing to do is to wait until you are asked.

Do have your elevator speech down, but...

You must be able to tell people who you are and what you do in seconds. Don't be afraid to make it interesting and fun! Working with a public speaking coach is a great way to learn how to create a killer elevator speech, but remember to keep it fluid and flexible depending on the situation—don't just press PLAY on the internal recorder.

Don't get too caught up in your smartphone.

You go to any networking event today and you see so many people standing alone texting or tweeting. They might as well be at home—I don't know why they bother to come out and be with other human beings at all!

Do show a genuine interest in what other people have to say.

Listen attentively to what the other person is saying. Ask them questions. What do they do? What do they need help with?

Don't ask for referrals from people you just met.

A friend told me about someone she had just met at a networking event who asked her for a referral right away. Obviously she was surprised and explained that she would need to get to know them better first.

Do take your business cards with you.

I'm astonished at the number of times I've met people only to have them say, "I forgot my business cards!" Always carry them with you; you never know who you're going to run into. One more important thing is to keep them up-to-date. Printing them is so inexpensive now, there is really no excuse.

Don't look like you just got out of bed.

I know that beauty shines from within, but it doesn't help if you haven't washed your hair in a month and you're wearing your favorite sweats. I always dress to impress, and so should you.

"Listen attentively to what the other person is saying. Ask them questions. What do they do? What do they need help with?"

Don't drink.

This is a *big* one, and I know many people will find this hard to do because most networking events have wine served and some even include a drink ticket. But drinking alcohol will impact the way you communicate and even your body language.

Do follow up with the people you meet after either by e-mail or social media.

Only about 10 percent of the people I meet at networking events follow up with me. That's pretty shocking, right? Send them a short e-mail or an invitation to connect on LinkedIn, Twitter, etc.

These tips are born out of my personal experiences attending hundreds of networking events. Networking has become a fundamental skill that every career professional, business or otherwise, has to master and be comfortable with. Ultimately my goal when networking is to expand my circle of professional contacts and see how we can help each other.

That's it—simple. Over the years I've been very lucky, and many of the people I've met over a glass of wine at an event are now my clients and even my friends. So take the time to master those front-line communication skills and see where they can take you.

Coaching Exercise 15

1. Do you have a good elevator speech? If not, now is the time to work on developing one. If you do, then work on making it even more concise and powerful.

2. What's your return on investment on networking at events? Do an analysis of your last few events. Have they actually led to business?

PART FOUR

PULLING IT ALL TOGETHER

CHAPTER 16

Take Charge of Your Speaking

*"The greater danger for most of us is not that our aim is too
high and we miss it, but that it is too low and we reach it."*
—Michelangelo

So you're almost at
the end of my
book—where do you
go from here? I want
this last chapter to be
about helping you pull
everything you've
learned in these pages
together to create an
action plan. Do you remember the learning outcomes you
mentioned in the beginning of the book? Did you meet
those? If you didn't do that exercise, it's not too late to go back
and think about it now. Too many people I meet meander
their way through business and life without a plan—you must
have a clear destination in mind. Imagine if you just went to
the airport on a whim without a destination and just went
anywhere. It may sound daring and adventurous, but in reality it would be a disaster. How would you know what to pack?
What if you didn't speak the language? What if it was a coun-
try in conflict? **You must have a destination in mind before
you begin your journey. It's the same if you want to be successful at anything, including public speaking.** Actually, in
all of my seminars and keynotes I always emphasize the
importance of execution. Without setting goals and taking
action to meet those goals, you will never realize your dreams.

Define your dream.

When all the problems of the world come crashing down on you (and let's face it, we all have days when that happens), it's your dream that propels you forward. So establish what that is—a clear vision of what you want to accomplish one, two, five, or ten years from now. What will your life look like? What kind of business do you want to build? Visualization really helps here—start by thinking in big, broad strokes. Let your mind wander free and find its dream. Don't be afraid if it feels too big; the bigger the better, I say. Remember that dreaming big requires courage. You must have the audacity to believe that you are capable of anything. *I recommend you read the book by David J. Schwartz in my recommended reading list. I love this book and reread it on a regular basis.*

> *"Remember that dreaming big requires courage. You must have the audacity to believe that you are capable of anything."*

Establish goals.

Now take that dream and divide it into bite-sized chunks so it becomes achievable. Remember to make sure your goals are *smart,* and use the section after this chapter to write them down. There is something powerful about writing down your goals—it makes them more tangible. Some of the common mistakes I see in goal-setting include setting too many goals, making them too vague, or making them too big.

> *"Keep going until you have achieved world-class public speaking skills—nothing less should be acceptable."*

Remember you can (and should) dream big, but your goals should be more realistic. In case you've forgotten, here's what I mean by *smart*:

S – Specific
M – Measurable
A – Attainable
R – Realistic
T – Time-Oriented

Take action.

This is where many people fail. They don't do anything. They expect that somehow their dream will magically materialize in their life without having to do any work. I have news for you—it doesn't work that way! **You make your dream happen. You have to take action to make your vision a reality. I often think that people don't realize how hard I have worked on my business to make it a success,** how much I've had to sacrifice. I'm sharing this with you so you appreciate that it didn't come easy to me, either. You need to make it happen.

"Remember the formula: Strategy + Execution = Success."

Build on your success.

As you learn, grow, and become more successful at speaking, you need to keep expanding your comfort zone and reevaluating your goals and even your dreams. Build on your success and never stop learning. I still invest my time and resources in courses, seminars, conferences, and coaching for self-development. So if you master one area, great! Move on to another and another. Keep going until you have achieved world-class public speaking skills—nothing less should be acceptable. Why? Because I believe in you, and I know that if I can do it, so can you. If you need some help along the way, you know where to reach me! Good luck.

Coaching Exercise 16

1. What is your dream, and how can public speaking help you to achieve it? Remember, think big!

2. Now take your dream and divide it up into bite-sized goals.

   a.

   b.

   c.

   d.

PART FIVE

QUICK TIP SHEETS

7

Things You Must Have in Your Speaking Tool Kit

I put this page in because I had no idea what I needed to have with me when I began speaking and I had to learn through trial and error. You get to learn from my mistakes! So whether you're a CEO or an entrepreneur just starting out, you should have the following items in your public speaking tool kit.

1. A well-written long speaker introduction or bio (hire a good writer if you don't write well; it's worth it for a great bio) and a well-written short speaker introduction or bio (you'll use this one more)
2. Current professional headshots (this does *not* mean severely airbrushed photos of you from ten years ago)
3. A presentation remote, or "clicker," as some people call it (plug-and-play USB-style is the type I use—I never leave home without it)
4. Flip chart/white board pens in a variety of colors
5. Flip chart paper (check if your venue will provide this)
6. A laptop, iPad, or tablet (for when you do use PowerPoint)
7. A stopwatch (or use an app on your cell phone that does the same thing)

7

Places to Look for
Speaking Opportunities

Here are seven places that you can start with to find speaking opportunities. Remember the more you practice, the better you will get. Just look them up online and approach them. Make sure your speaking tool kit is in place first, and good luck!

1. International clubs and membership organizations
2. Chambers of commerce or boards of trade
3. Women's organizations
4. Networking groups
5. Professional organizations (e.g., engineers, accountants, etc.)
6. Within your own organization—leading projects, staff orientations, and training. Now is the time to step up and speak out!
7. High Schools, colleges, and universities

Ways to Improve Your Next PowerPoint Presentation

Here are seven ways to immediately improve your next digital presentation to any audience. I put this checklist in because I see so many people make these mistakes!

1. Don't read from the slides.
2. Go back and read number 1 again—*it's that important.*
3. Keep your design consistent with your branding.
4. Don't crowd each line with too much information.
5. Leave enough white space on each slide for the "eyes to rest."
6. Edit down the number of slides.
7. Add large images and video for greater impact.

Things You MUST Check Before You Give Any Conference Keynote

Here's a quick list of seven things you must check before any speech or presentation in front of a medium- to large-sized group.

1. Your technology is working.
2. You have a backup plan in case your technology fails anyway. (I've been there, so trust me on this one!)
3. Your microphone is working—try it on, move around, and do a sound check.
4. Use a mirror or trusted colleague to check your teeth and your face for any other weird bits and bobs.
5. Will there be a podium? A stage? Get a feel for the speaking area.
6. Check the layout of the room. Is it theatre-style or rounds? Square or L-shaped? Do this so you can maximize eye contact.
7. Make sure the person introducing you has the most up-to-date version of your speaker introduction, not something they just downloaded from the Internet or made up on the spur of the moment (been there, too).

7 Questions to Ask Before You Hire an Executive Speech Coach

Here are seven things you must ask before you hire a public speaking coach, executive speech coach, or presentation skills trainer.

1. Do they have a website? Check it out before you talk to them.
2. Do they have a profile on LinkedIn with endorsements? Check it out and read the testimonials.
3. Are they an experienced speaker themselves? Can you see sample videos and photos from events? How can they help you speak if they don't speak themselves?
4. Are they considered an expert by the media? Are media appearances mentioned on their website? This goes to their ability to help you build your platform and raise your profile.
5. What did they do before they did this? Goes to credibility.
6. Are they doing this part-time or full-time? Do they have a successful business, or is this just a hobby? Will they still be available to help you one or two years from now?
7. Do they specialize in this area or are they dabbling in a variety of different things? Are they a coach or consultant of everything under the sun, or are they truly an expert in one area with a depth of knowledge and experience to match?

Recommended Reading

Here is a list of twelve of my favorite books in the business and self-help genre. Actually, it was hard cutting down the list to just twelve. These books aren't just full of hard facts; some of them are also very inspiring, and I believe that reading them has impacted my life greatly. I hope you enjoy reading these books as much as I have.

Brendon Burchard, *The Millionaire Messenger: Make a Difference and a Fortune Sharing Your Advice*

Jack Canfield, *The Success Principles*™

Deepak Chopra, *The Seven Spiritual Laws of Success: A Practical Guide to the Fulfillment of Your Dreams*

Arlene Dickinson, *Persuasion: A New Approach to Changing Minds*

Darren Hardy, *The Compound Effect*

Michael Hyatt, *Platform: Get Noticed in a Noisy World*

Guy Kawasaki, *The Art of the Start: The Time-Tested, Battle-Hardened Guide for Anyone Starting Anything*

Peter Legge, *The Runway of Life*

John C. Maxwell, *Leadership Gold: Lessons I've Learned from a Lifetime of Leading*

Tom Peters, *The Brand You 50 (Reinventing Work): Fifty Ways to Transform Yourself from an 'Employee' into a Brand That Shouts Distinction, Commitment, and Passion!*

David J. Schwartz, *The Magic of Thinking Big*

Robin Sharma, *The Leader Who Had No Title: A Modern Fable on Real Success in Business and in Life*

About the Author

Narges Nirumvala is the founder and CEO of ExecutiveSpeak Coaching International. She works with corporate leaders, association executives, elected community officials, and high-performance teams to help them find their authentic voice, craft persuasive content, and communicate with confidence in any public speaking situation from boardroom presentations to conference keynotes.

She is a columnist for *Entrepreneurial Woman* magazine, and her writing on the subject has been circulated to 106 countries worldwide. Narges is often called upon by the media as an expert in her field. She has appeared numerous times in and on print, radio, and television. She is also a much-sought-after professional keynote speaker and seminar leader. Narges is an energizing, inspiring, and empowering speaker for conferences, AGMs, and other corporate functions.

Narges believes passionately in giving back and has served on numerous not-for-profit boards over the years. She is a mentor with the prestigious Leaders of Tomorrow® program through the Vancouver Board of Trade. She was a finalist for the Women of Worth (WOW)™ Mompreneur of the Year Award and Spirit, Success & Soul Award. She was also one of only a handful of people in Vancouver short-listed for the Expert Category of the North America Small Business Influencer Awards.

You can keep in touch with Narges through her online profiles:
Web: ExecutiveSpeak.com
Facebook: Facebook.com/ExecutiveSpeak
Twitter: @NargesNirumvala
YouTube: Youtube.com/NargesNirumvala

About Narges Nirumvala's
Keynotes and Seminars

Make your next event more memorable and powerful by booking Executive Speech Coach Narges Nirumvala to speak.

From the moment Narges Nirumvala steps onto your stage, the sparks begin to fly as she ignites the audience with her energy. Her presentations are practical and filled with "how to's" and "why to's" that show attendees how to go beyond average and shine—at work and in life.

She is motivational, inspirational, uplifting, and energizing, and she moves people to action by sharing personal stories, strategies, and insights to help make goals and dreams. Her experience in coaching people to peak performance provides a foundation for empowering others to reach their true potential.

Her powerful and interactive keynotes, workshops, and strategy sessions give the audience essential tools to take their vision—whether it relates to their career, business, or life—and create a realistic plan that moves them to action.

Narges's audience includes corporations, associations, conferences, retreats, and workshops.

To book Narges to speak at your next event, e-mail narges@executivespeak.com.

About Narges Nirumvala's
Executive Speech Coaching

Narges Nirumvala has quickly established herself as one of the top executive speech coaches in North America and works with executives, entrepreneurs, community leaders, politicians, and corporations to take their public speaking and presentation skills to the next level.

If you're thinking about hiring Narges, then you are already an accomplished, driven, and successful individual. **You need a trusted advisor who understands the importance of getting your message across and speaking the language of leadership.**

If you are looking for high-caliber executive speech coaching and sales presentation skills training, then you will not find anyone else with Narges's passion, knowledge, credentials, and expertise. Narges has a unique system that includes writing and developing persuasive content, as well as working on your delivery and understanding how it integrates into your unique situation, communication, marketing, and sales strategy.

Because Narges works almost exclusively with top-tier clients, she understands the tremendous pressure they are under, and their need for immediate results, and she promises confidentiality and discretion.

To contact Narges about her one-on-one coaching and corporate training, e-mail: narges@executivespeak.com.